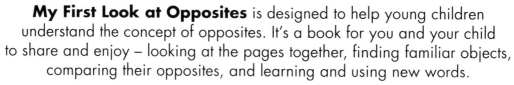

A Dorling Kindersley Book

Note to Parents

My First Look at Opposites is designed to help young children understand the concept of opposites. It's a book for you and your child to share and enjoy – looking at the pages together, finding familiar objects, comparing their opposites, and learning and using new words.

Have fun with opposites!

Senior Editor Jane Yorke	*Photography* Stephen Oliver
Art Editor Toni Rann	*Additional photography*
Designer Jane Coney	Michael Dunning, Karl Shone
Editorial Director Sue Unstead	*Series Consultant* Neil Morris
Art Director Colin Walton	

First published in Great Britain in 1990
by Dorling Kindersley Publishers Limited,
9 Henrietta Street, London WC2E 8PS

Reprinted 1990, 1992, 1993, 1996

Copyright © 1990 Dorling Kindersley Limited, London

A CIP catalogue record for this book is available from the British Library.

ISBN 0-86318-463-4

Phototypeset by Flairplan Phototypesetting Ltd, Ware, Hertfordshire
Reproduced in Hong Kong by Bright Arts
Printed in Italy by L.E.G.O.

· MY · FIRST · LOOK · AT ·

Opposites

DK

DORLING KINDERSLEY
London • New York • Stuttgart

Big and little

shoes

leaves

cars

crabs

tomatoes

dolls

Thick and thin

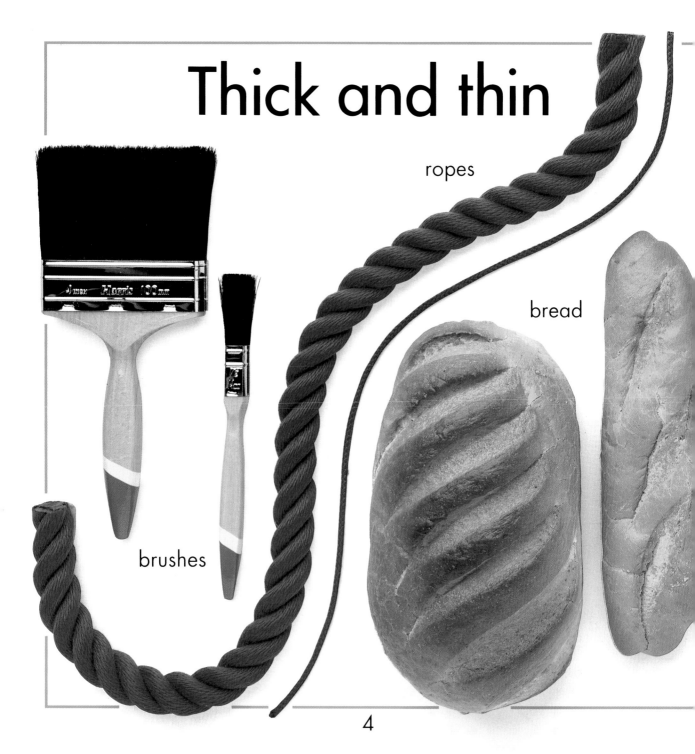

ropes

bread

brushes

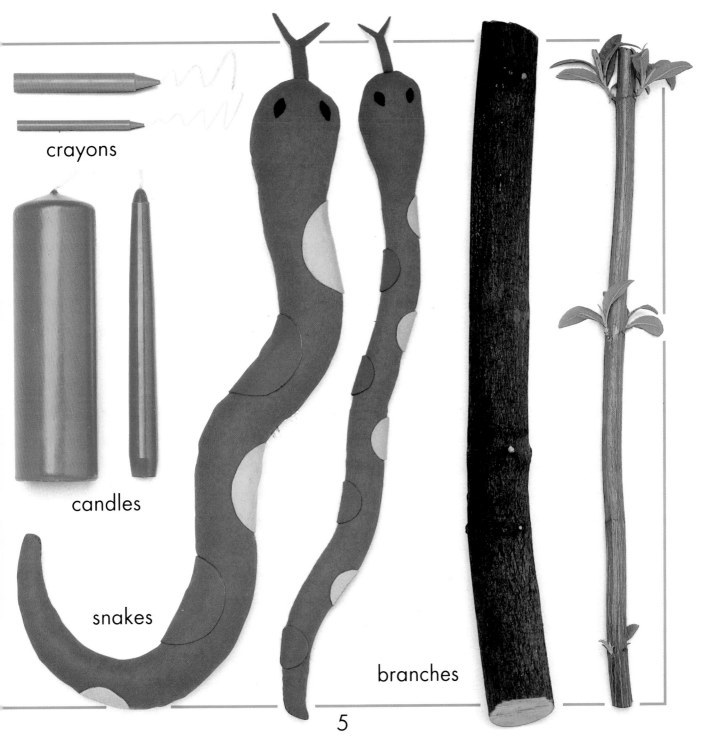

crayons

candles

snakes

branches

5

Long and short

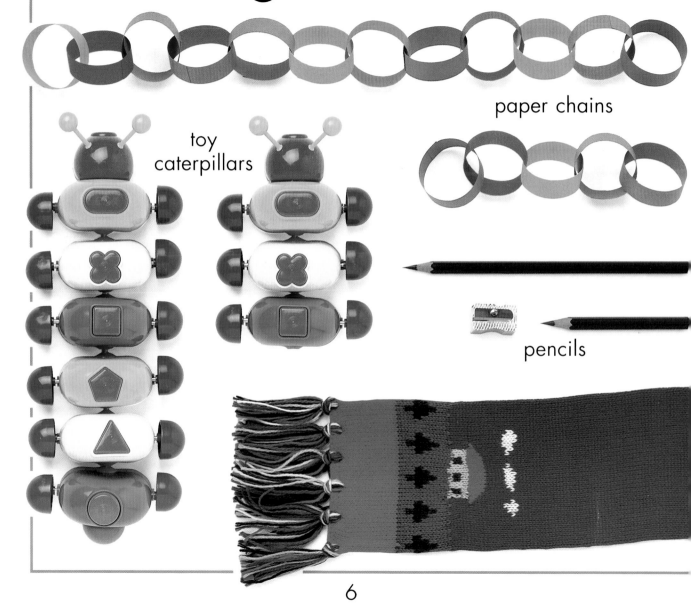

paper chains

toy
caterpillars

pencils

6

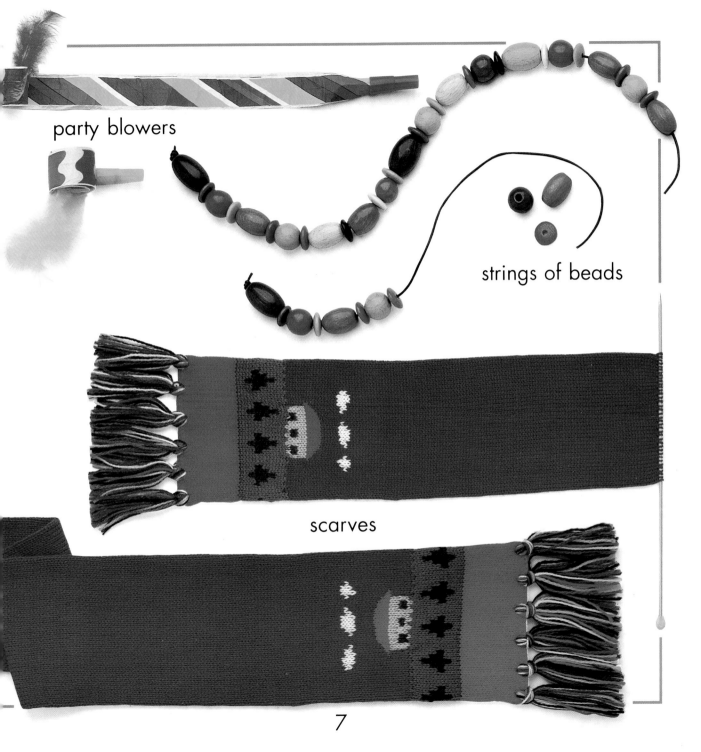

party blowers

strings of beads

scarves

In and out

pilot

sand-castle

tortoise

snail

jack-in-the-box

Up and down

crane

puppet

ladder

train

11

Full and empty

biscuit tin

bird's nest

toy box

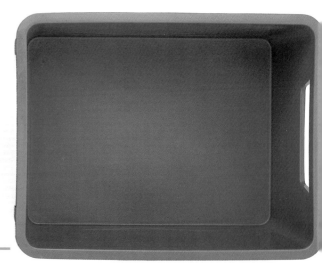

tube of paint

fruit bowl

sweet jar

glass

Front and back

clock

tiger

truck

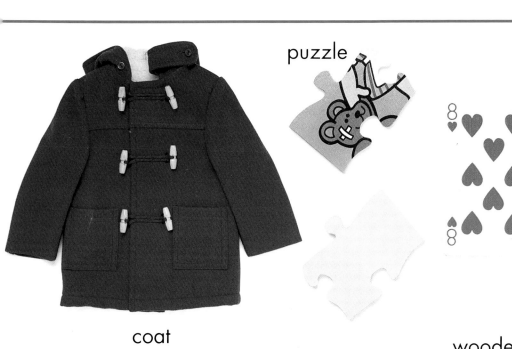

puzzle

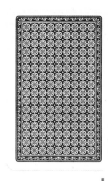

card

coat

wooden doll

15

Open and closed

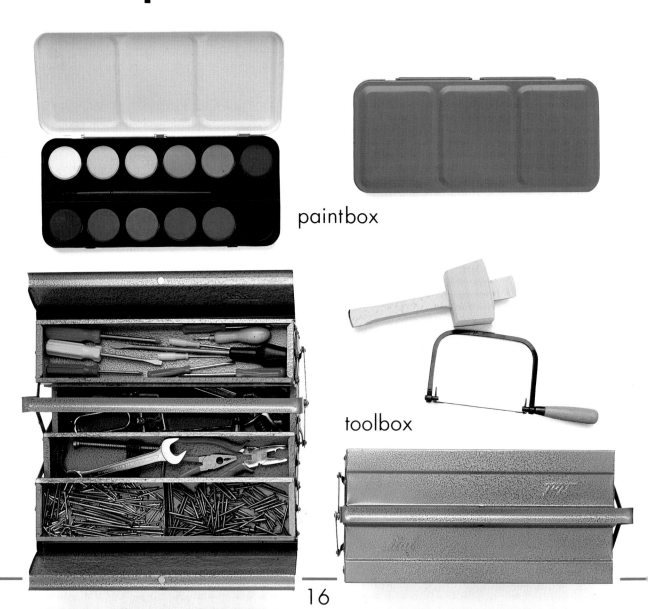

paintbox

toolbox

jewellery box

handbag

door